KINDER KOLLEGE
Science Smart Start

L. M. Logan
Patrice Juah
Ophelia S. Lewis

Village Tales Publishing

MINNEAPOLIS, MN

Copyright © 2020 by Liberia Literary Society
All rights reserved. No part of this publication may be reproduced, distributed or transmitted in any form or by any means, without prior written permission.

Village Tales Publishing
www.villagetalespublishing.com
www.oass.villagetalespublishing.com
www.villagetalespublishing.com/childrensbooks

Book Cover by OASS
ISBN: 9781944508311
LCCN: 2020905089

A Liberia Literary Society Educational Project

Printed in the USA

This book belongs to:

_____

How to care for your book.

1. Read with clean hands.

2. Turn pages carefully.

3. Keep your book in your bookbag when you're not reading it.

4. Keep your book close to you when reading, so that you don't drop it.

5. Use a bookmark to save your page in a book.

6. Keep your book away from food and drinks.

7. Only draw, write, and color where instructed to.

8. Keep your book away from younger siblings and pets.

Primary Handwriting Guidelines

The first thing I do is always the same,
I pick up my pencil and write my name.

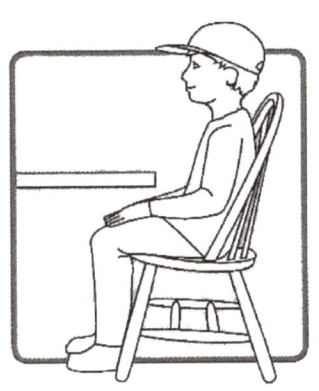  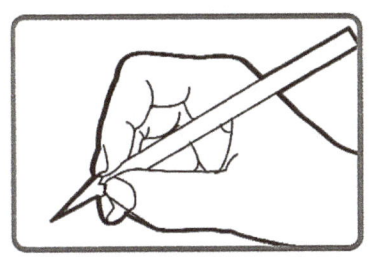

Sit down and place book flat in front of you.

Use your helper hand to hold the paper down while writing.

Correctly hold your pencil; only move the fingers when writing.

Contents

Science and Scientists 7
Different Areas of Science 8
Scientific Methods 9
Scientists' Tools & Instruments 10
Weather Measurement Tools 11
Weather in Liberia 15
Earth Science 16
The Rock Cycle 18
Landforms 19
Physical Science 21
Simple Machines 23
Force & Motion 24
What is speed? 25
What is gravity? 27
What is a magnet? 28
Energy Science 29
Energy Sources 30
Natural Energy Resources 33
How We Use Energy 35
Life Science 36
Living vs Non-living 36
Plants 40
Plants in Our Lives 43
Animals 44
Animal characteristics 46
Animal Babies Grow Up 49
My Body 50
Our Five Senses 52
Things we can do 53
Healthy Habits 54
Prevent Malaria 58
Things I Like About Myself 60

Science and Scientists

What is science?

Science is the study of our world around us.

A Scientist is someone who studies how a specific thing works.

Different Areas of Science

Human and Animal Life

The Earth

Plant

Outer Space

The Environment

Energy and Motion

Scientific Methods

Scientific methods is a way for scientists to study and learn things. This help them come up with an answer.

What do scientists do?

Scientist Activities

Research → they ask a question → they form a hypothesis (guess) → they test and experiment → they record their observation → they come to a conclusion → Research

Scientists' Tools & Instruments

scientist   beaker
magnet   balance
methods   mircroscope
            magnifying glass

scientists

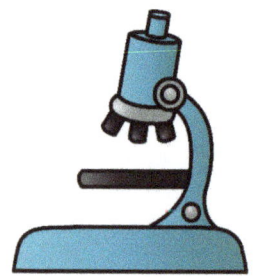
microscope

magnet

beaker

magnifying glass

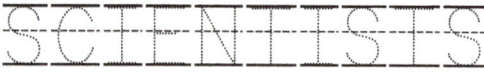
SCIENTISTS

BALANCE

BEAKER

MAGNET

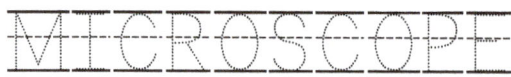
METHODS

MICROSCOPE

MAGNIFYING GLASS

balance

Weather Measurement Tools

thermometer — an instrument for measuring temperature.

THERMOMETER

an instrument for measuring the quality of water that falls to earth; rain, smow, hail

rain gauge

RAIN GAUGE

wind sock — shows the direction of the wind.

WIND SOCK

A meteorologist studies the atmosphere and weather.

Meteorology is a science that deals with the atmosphere, weather and weather forecasting.

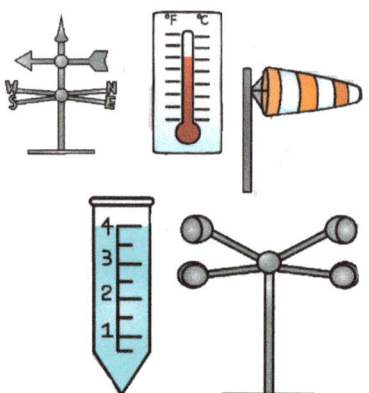

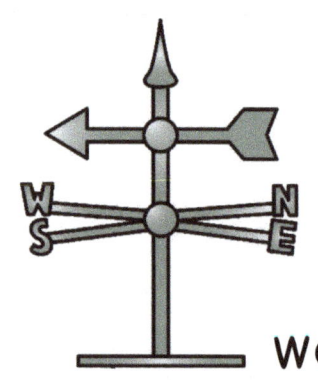 shows which way the wind is blowing.

weather vane

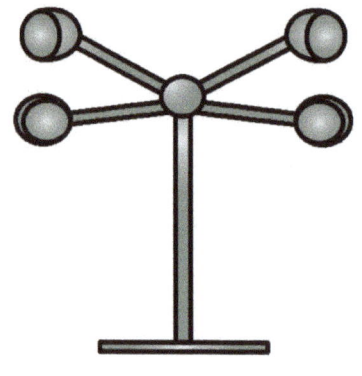 an instrument for measuring the speed of the wind.

anemometer

Weather Tracking

sunny	cloudy	snowy	stormy	rainy	windy

How many days were sunny?

How many days were windy?

How many days were snowy?

How many days were rainy?

How many days were cloudy?

How many days were stormy?

Weather Word Match-up

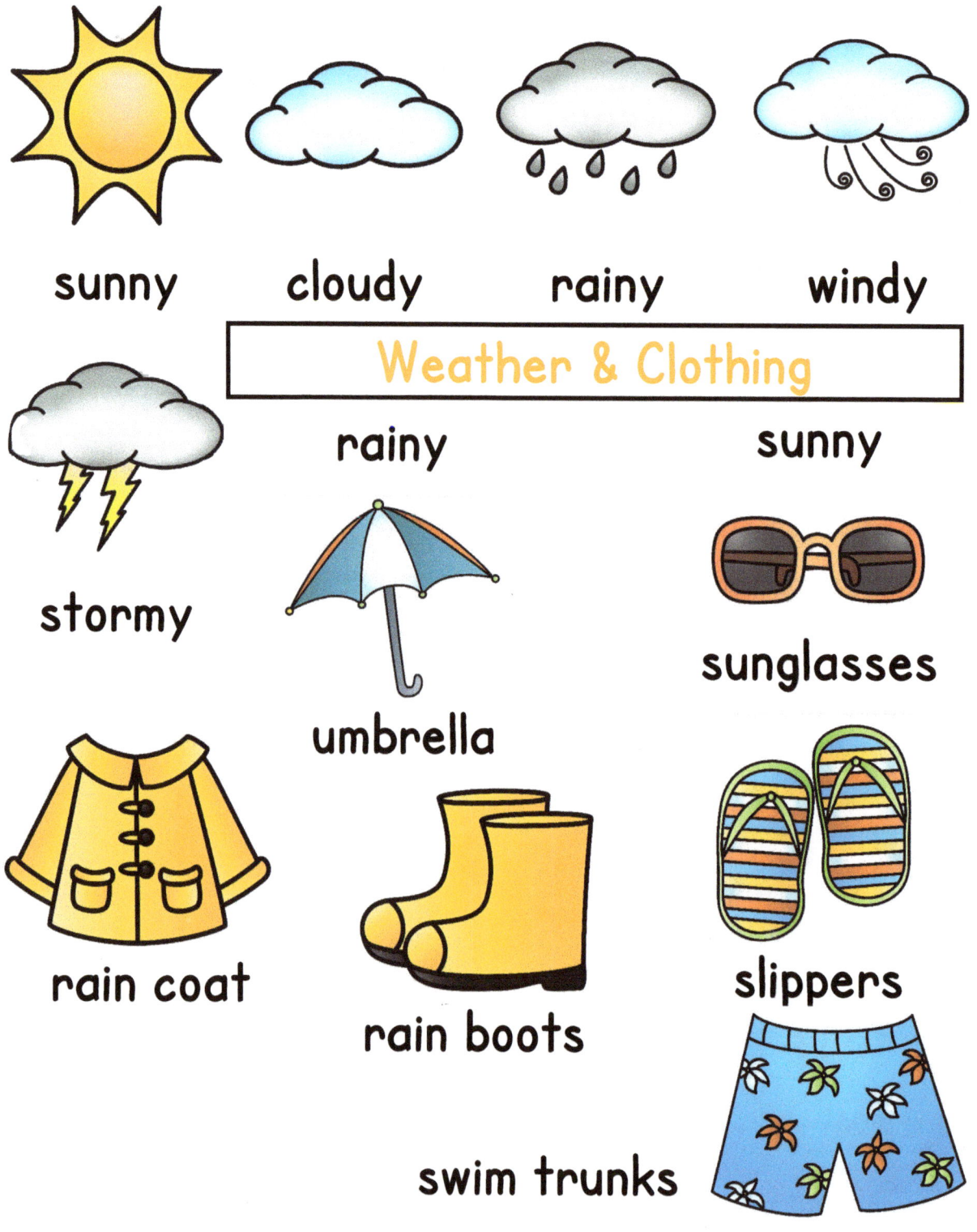

Weather in Liberia

Rainy Season	Dry Season
May to October	November to April

The Water Cycle

condensation
precipitation
evaporation
accumulation

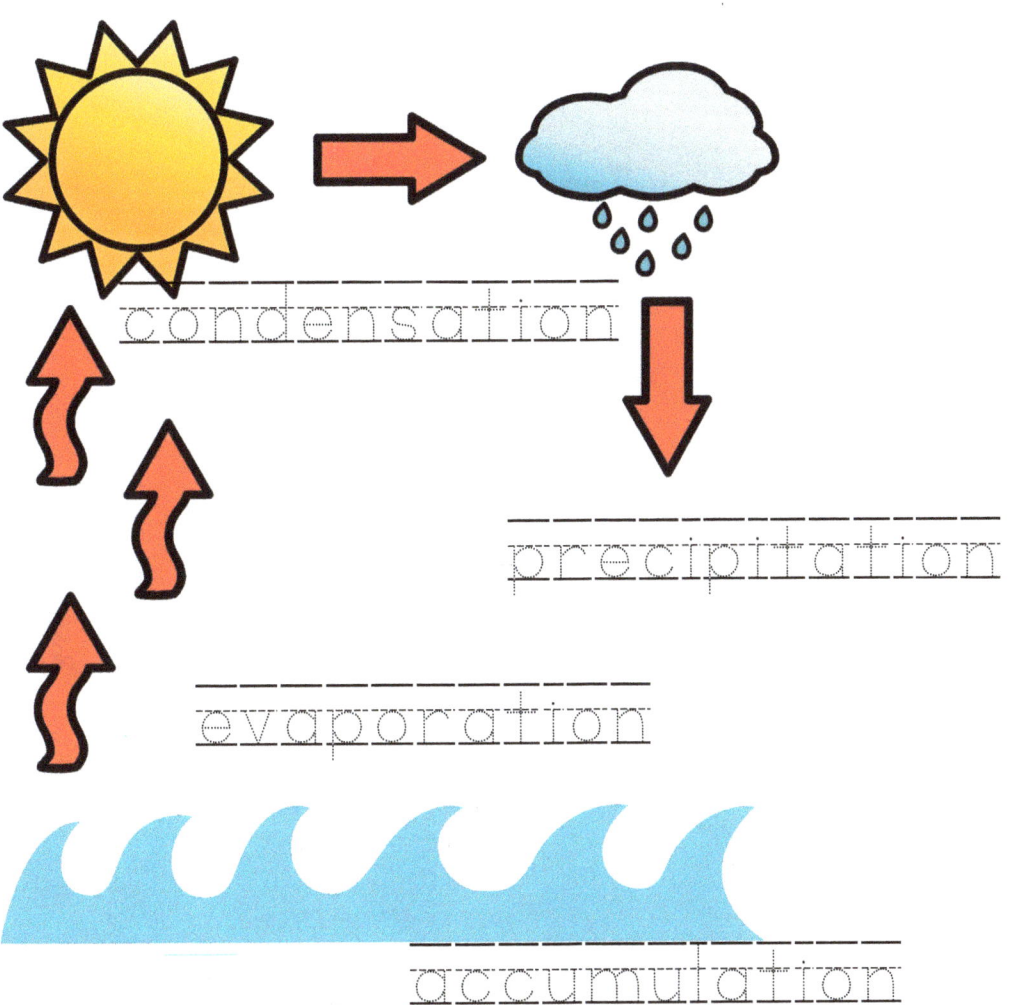

Earth Science

Earth's Layers

We love our planet Earth.
We recycle to keep it neat and clean.

Earth's Composition

land   air   water

Types of Soil

clay

silt

sand

Soil layers

- humus
- top soil
- sub soil
- parent material
- bedrock

The Rock Cycle

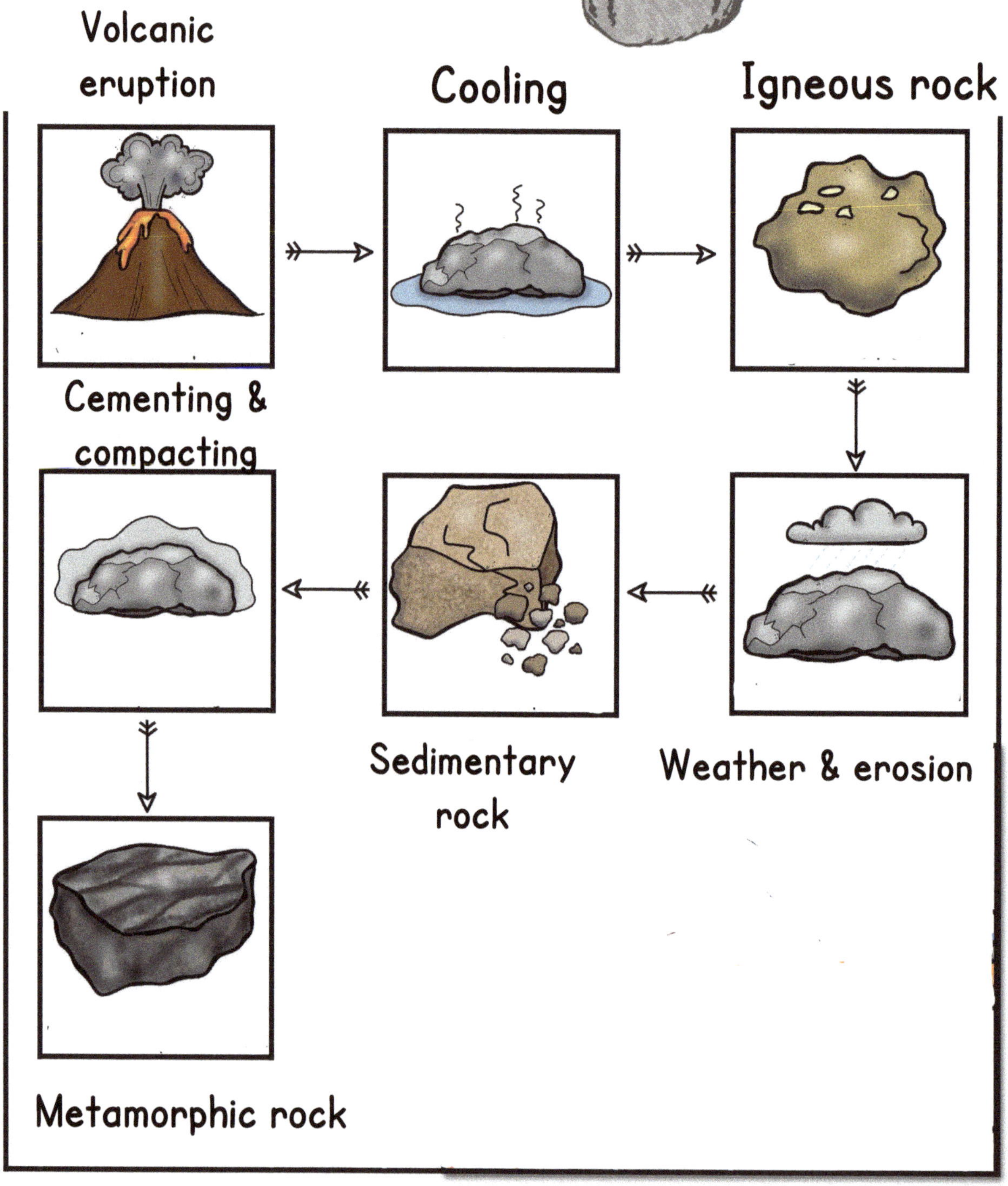

Volcanic eruption → Cooling → Igneous rock → Weather & erosion → Sedimentary rock → Cementing & compacting → Metamorphic rock

Landforms

mountains

pond

canyon

cave

island

river

volcano

cliff

lake

Physical Science

21

Things that are...

Light   Soft

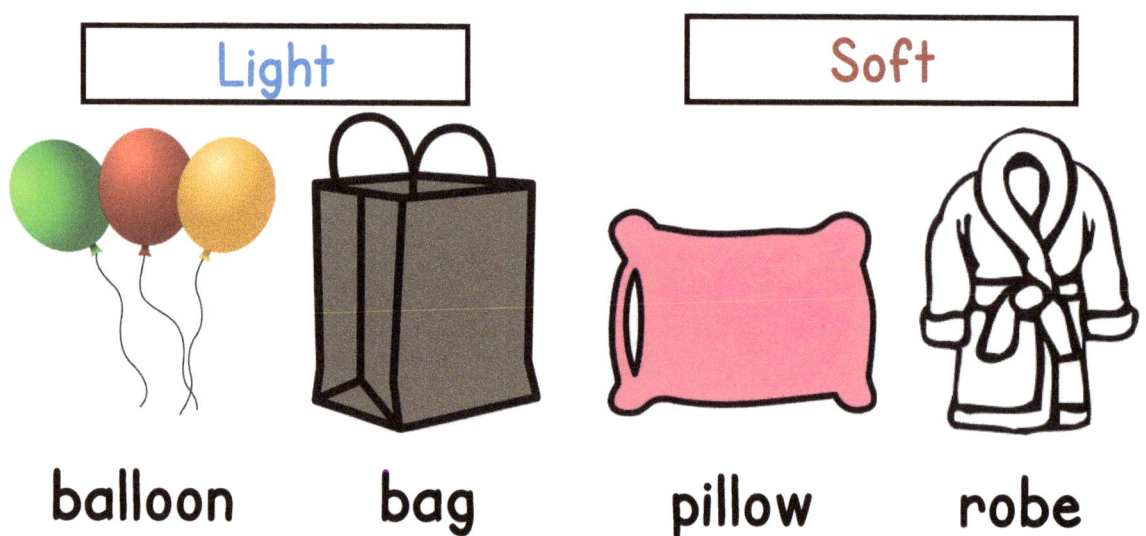

balloon   bag   pillow   robe

Things that are...

Heavy   Rough

bus   horse   rope   broom

Simple Machines	are used to make	Big Machines

wheel & axle

lever

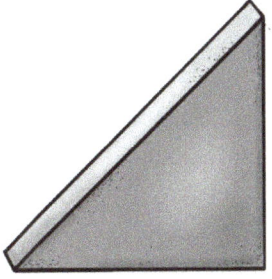
inclined plane

pulley

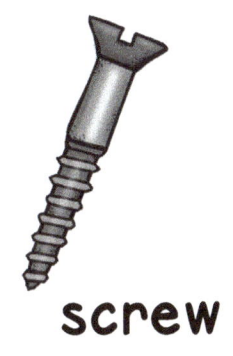
screw

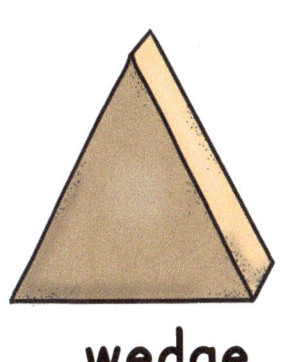
wedge

vocabulary

force	move	speed
gravity	ramp	magnet
pole	repel	attract

Force & Motion

| How do things move? | By force. |

FORCE is a push or pull that may make something move.

Fun on the merry-go-round.

What is speed?

SPEED is how quickly or slowly something moves.

Number 1-5, from slowest speed to the fastest speed.

☐ taxi

☐ plane

☐ girl

☐ truck

☐ bike

25

At the Playground

Objects can move in a straight line, zig zag, up and down, back and forth, round and round, and fast and slow.

back and forth

fast and slow

A merry-go-round goes round and round.

up & down

What is gravity?

GRAVITY is the force that pulls things toward the ground.

water in a waterfall flow

sliding down the slide

What is a ramp?

A ramp is a slanting surface connecting a lower level to a higher level.

Objects can move in a straight line, zig zag, up and down, back and forth, round and round, and fast and slow.

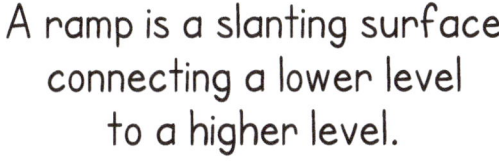

up & down

What is a magnet?

A magnet is an object that attracts some kinds of metals.

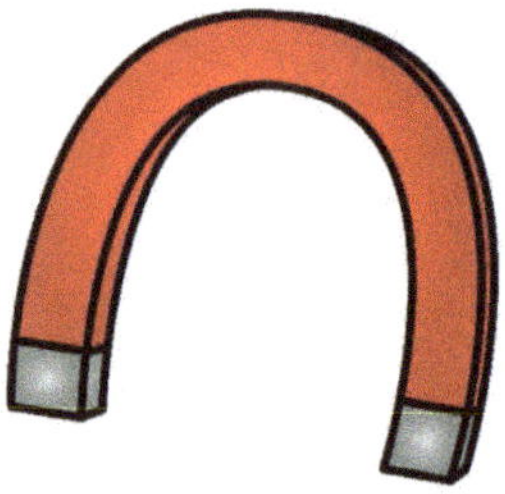

A magnet has two poles. The poles are at each end of a magnet. Each magnet has a north pole and a south pole. North poles attract south poles.

Magnetic

- can
- needle 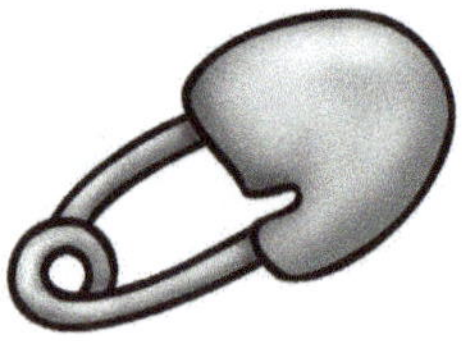
- nails
- pin

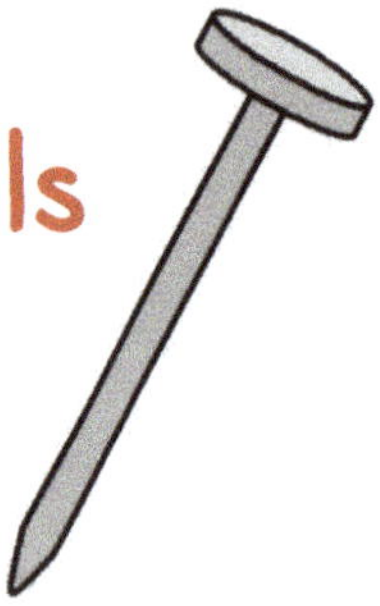

Not Magnetic

- highlighter
- paper 
- shell 
- rug

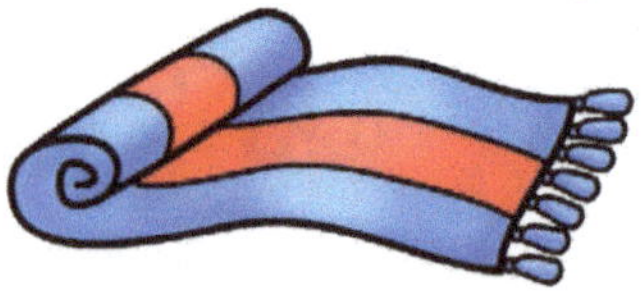

Energy Science

Energy is something that is needed to make things happen.

Electrical Energy

Elastic Energy

Light Energy

Kinetic Energy

Sound Energy

Chemical Energy

Muscle Energy

Energy Sources

Where do we get our energy from?

The Super Duper Sun   The most important source of enegry is the sun.

- Warmth
- Light
- Energy
- Power
- Life
- Food

What would the Earth be like if there was no sun? What would happen to plants, animals, and people?

 No Sun

We Need Energy To Live

I get energy from the sun.

I get energy from animals. I get energy from plants.

Energy Chain
The path energy takes to get from one living thing to another.

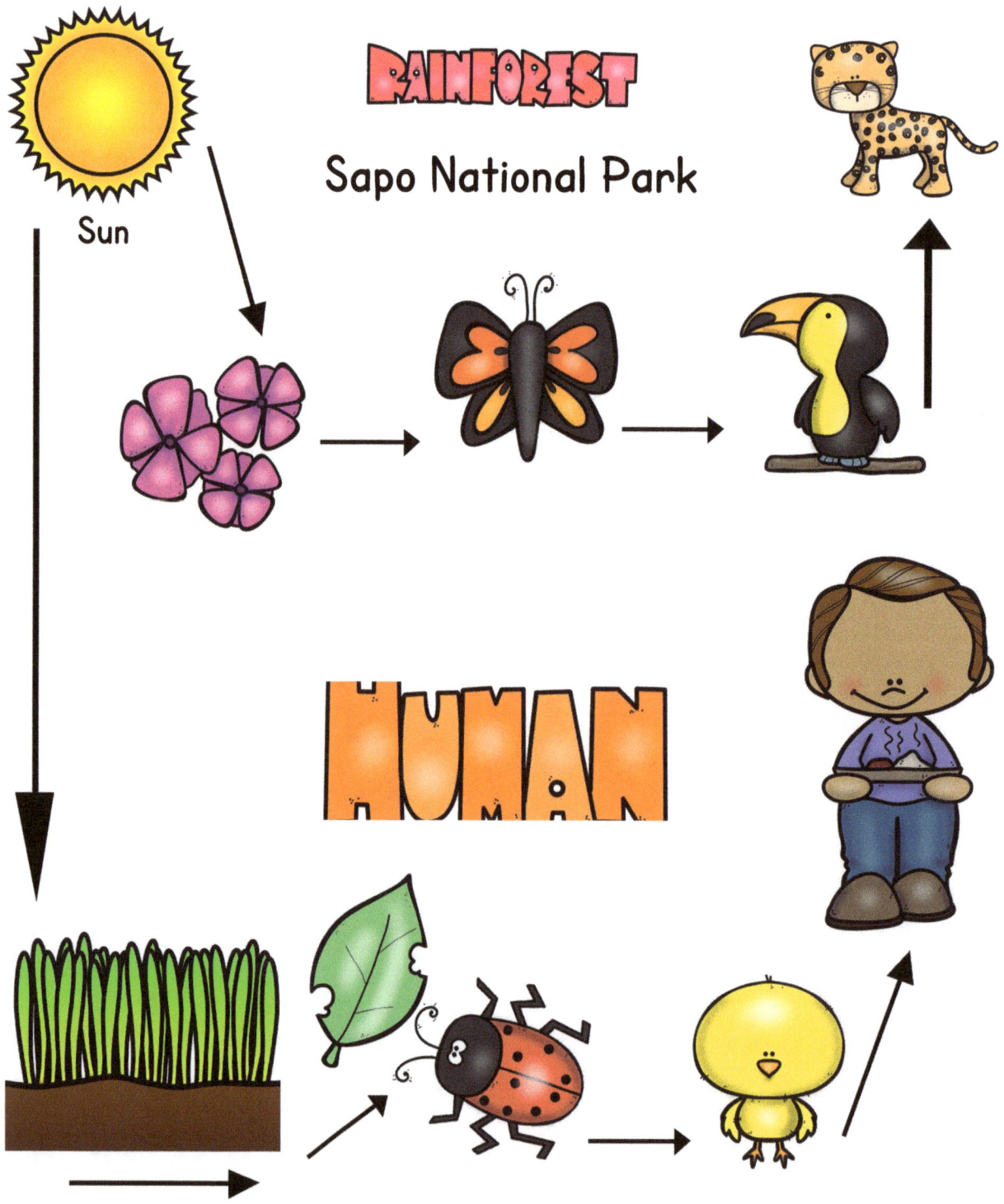

Natural Energy Resources

Nature provides us with energy in the form of natural resources. Natural resources can be living or nonliving. Not all natural resources last forever. There are 2 different types of natural energy sources.

Renewable Energy

Renewable energy resources can be replaced. They are produced by nature again and again.

Solar
Energy from the sun changed to electricity.

Wind
Energy from wind changed to electricity

Hydroelectric Power
Energy from moving water changed to electricity.

Renewable Energy

Plants
Energy in the form of food.

Animals
Energy in the form of food for other animals and humans.

Non-renewable Energy

Non-renewable energy resources cannot be replaced in our lifetime. They take thousands, even millions, of years to replace.

Gasoline **Natural Gas** **Iron Ore** **Oil**

Coal

*fossil fuels – decayed plants and animals that have been changed to oil, coal, and natural gas

How We Use Energy

Energy in our lives.

Life Science

Living vs Non-living

Animals, plants, and people are living. They need three things to survive: food, water, and air.

food

water

air

Nonliving things **do not** grow.
They **do not** need food, water, or air.

teddy bear

hat

pickup

Living things **grow**.
They **need** food, water, or air.

grasshopper

girl

boy

cow

fish

plant

owl

bee

The sun gives us heat. Without the heat from the sun, we would not be able to survive on Earth.

Gifts of the sun

Plants use the sun to grow and help make food.

food

Things that protect us from the sun.

The sun gives us light. Light helps us to see during the day.

sunglasses

water   hat

Plants

All plants grow and change. A plant begins its life inside of a seed. Soon it sprouts from the seed and rises from the soil as a seedling. Finally, the seedling will grow and change into a full grown plant.

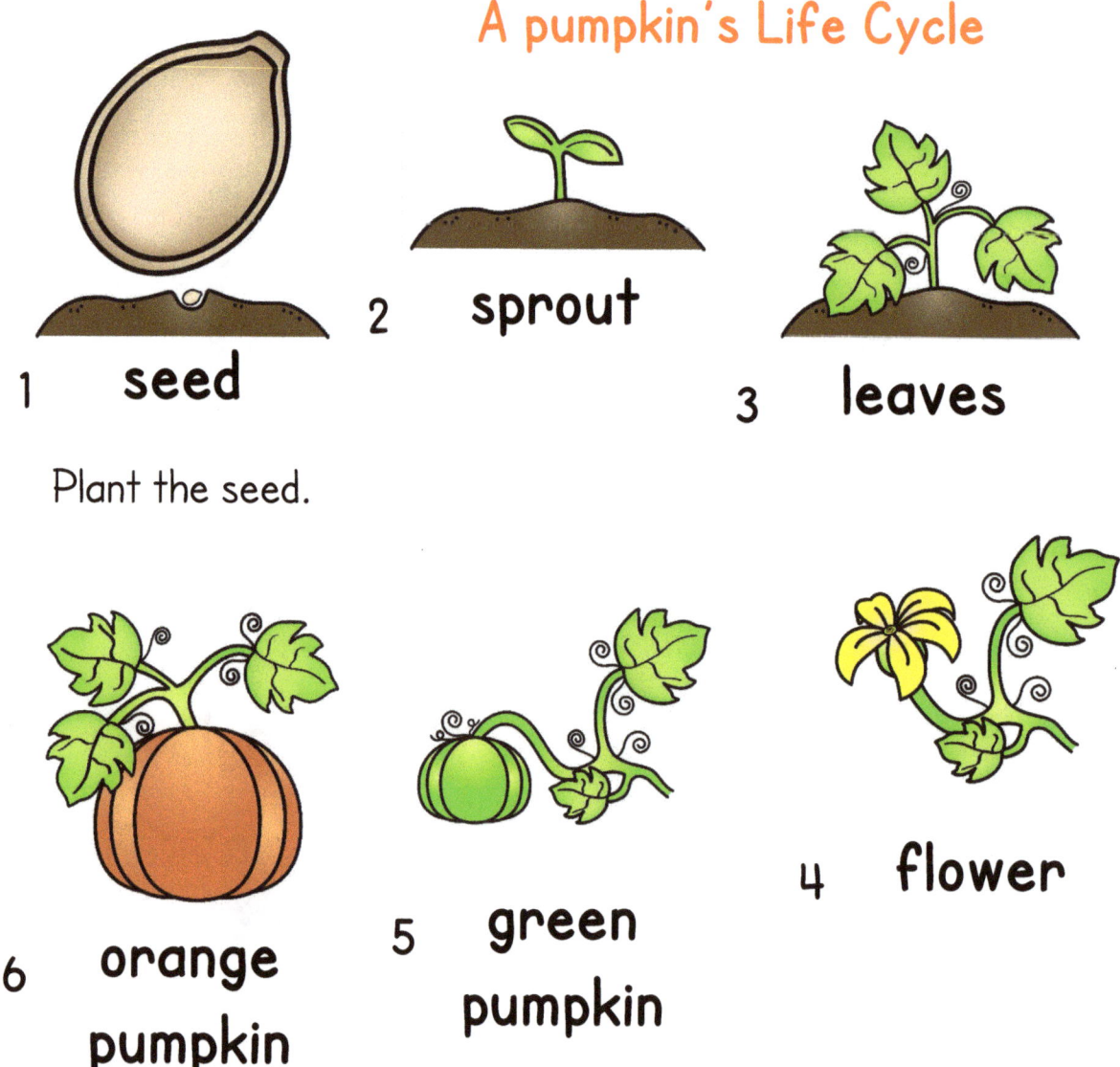

A pumpkin's Life Cycle

1 seed

2 sprout

3 leaves

Plant the seed.

4 flower

5 green pumpkin

6 orange pumpkin

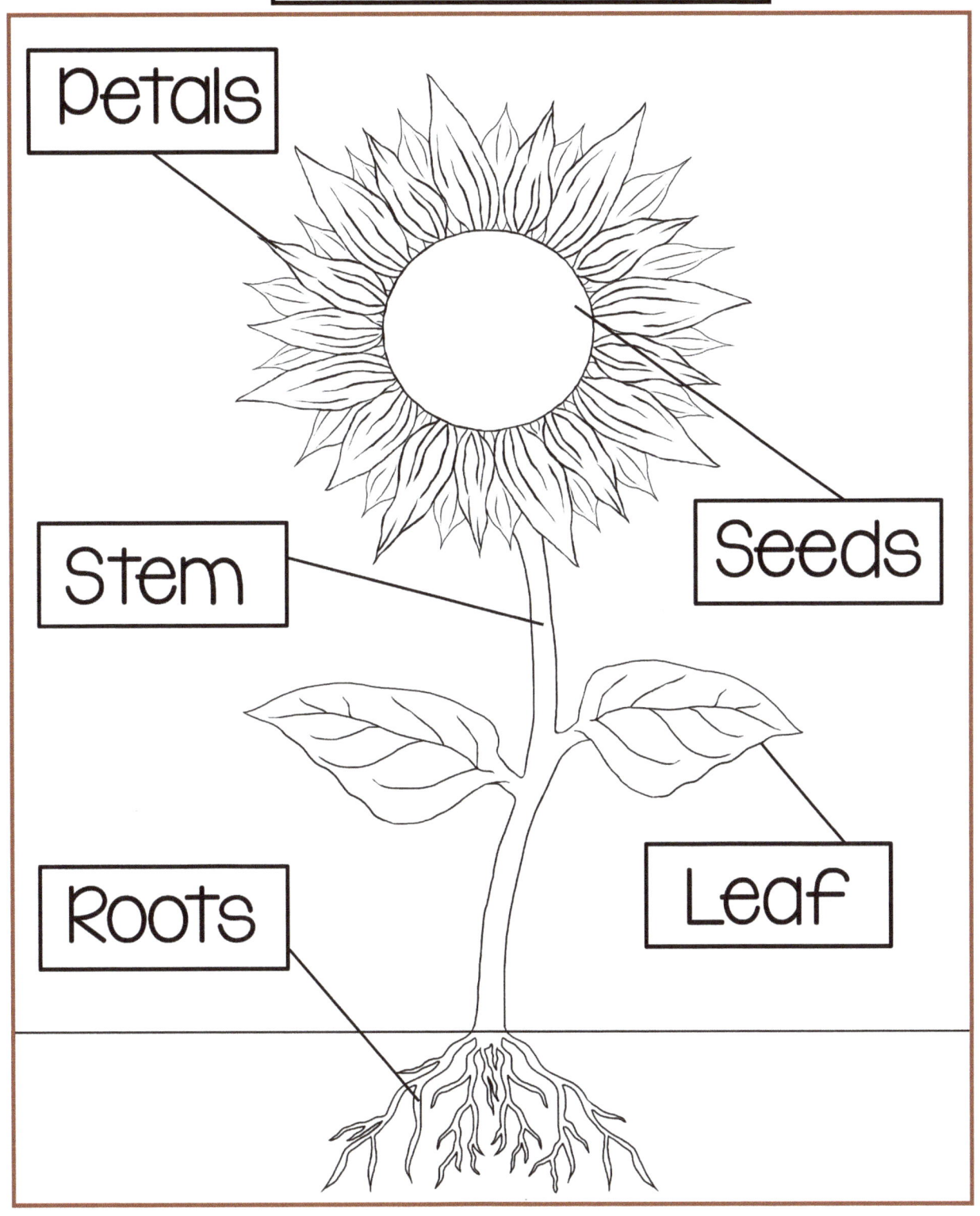

Eating Plants

When we eat  eddos

We are eating the root

When we eat  onions

We are eating the stem

When we eat  corn

We are eating the seed

When we eat potato greens

We are eating the leaves

When we eat  okra

We are eating the flower

Plants in Our Lives

ear mouth
eyes tail
nose paw

Animals

Doggie Body

Crab Parts

Crabs have 10 legs. The front two legs have claws. Crabs can swim. The back two legs help crabs swim. Crabs have two eyestalks. Any eyestalk may be long. Crabs have a hard outer shell. Crabs can shed their shell as they grow.

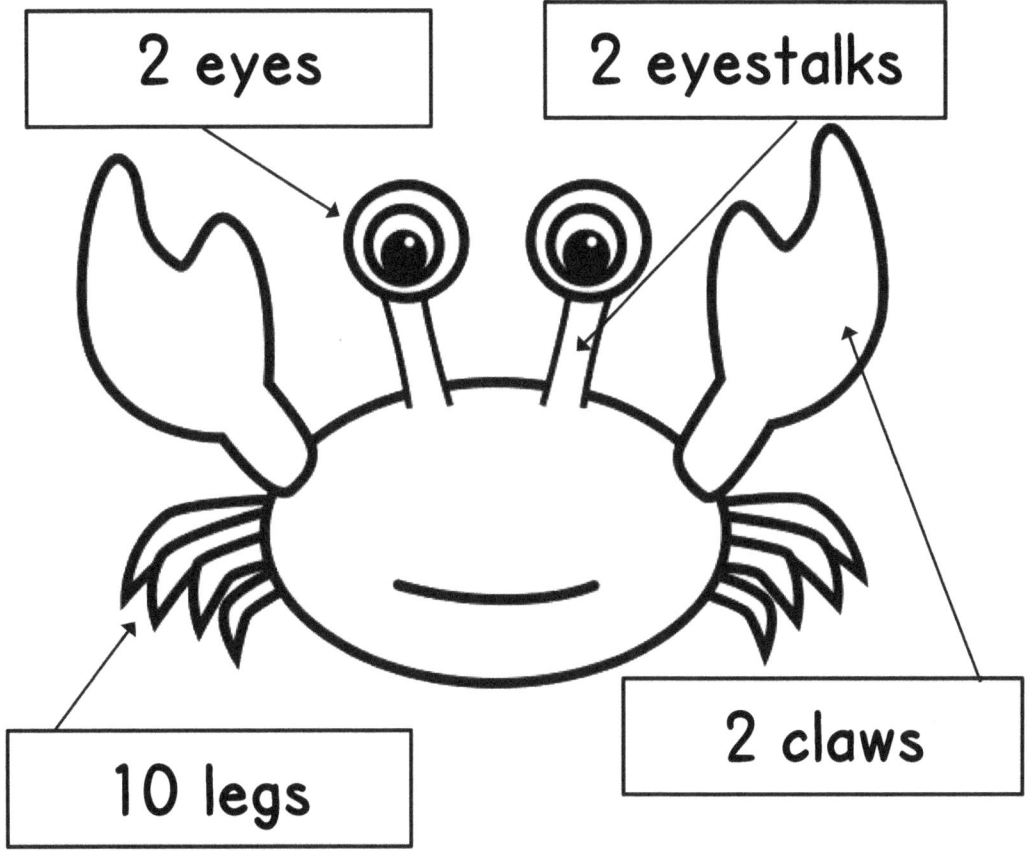

Animal characteristics

47

Animal Movement

Some animals fly.

mosquito   bird

bee

Some animals swim.

Some animals hop.

grasshopper

bunny

frog

alligator   fish

octopus

48

Animal Babies Grow Up

| calf |  cow |  chick |  chicken |

| foal |  horse |  lamb |  sheep |

| piglet |  pig |  kid |  goat |

How many of these animal babies have you seen?

49

My Body

Our Body

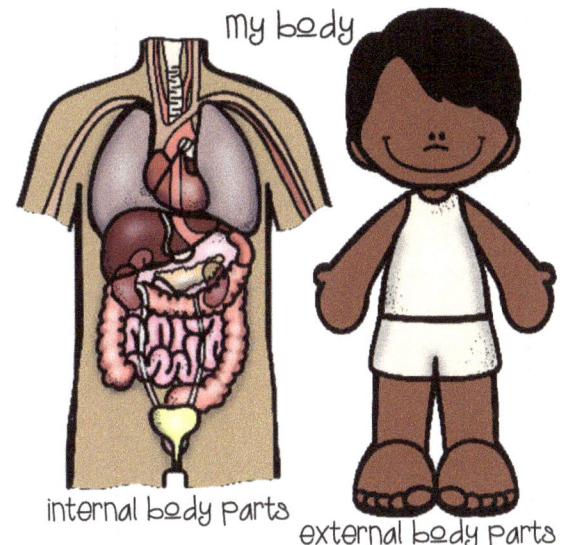

The bones in my body make up my skeleton. My skeleton gives me shape. It protects the soft part inside me. I have over 200 bones.

| blood | bones | skeleton |

The muscles help me move by pulling the bones in my body. The best way to keep my muscles strong is to exercise everyday.

| oxygen | muscles | lungs |

My heart and lungs work together. When I breathe in, my lungs take in oxygen. Oxygen goes into my blood. Then my heart pumps the blood to all the different parts of my body.

| spine | brain | nerves |

My brain keeps my body alive. It helps me move and think. It tells my nerves what to do. These nerves go down my spine to each part of my body. My body works because of my brain.

| Our Five Senses | We explore the world using our five senses. |

I see with my eyes.
sight

I hear with my ears.
hearing

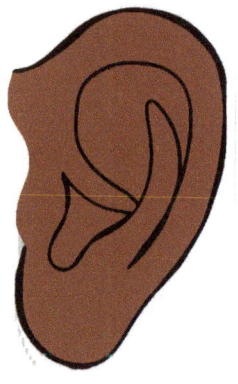

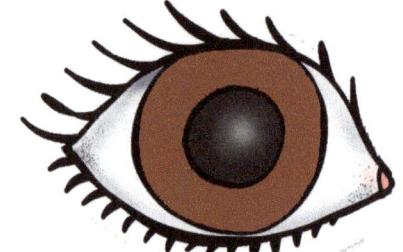

I touch and feel things with my hands.
touch

I smell with my nose.
smell

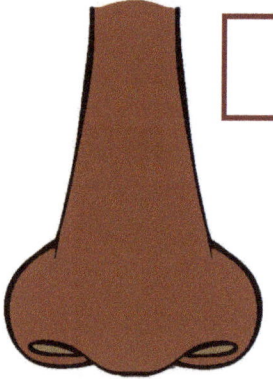

The taste buds on my tongue let me enjoy my favorite foods.
taste

Things we can do...

during the Day

look at a rainbow
go to school
ride a bike
play at the beach

Things we can do...

at Night

sleep
catch lightning bugs
look at the stars
use a flashlight

Healthy Habits

Bathroom Rules

My Healthy Habits

I exercise.
I eat healthy food.
I go to bed early.
I drink lots of water.

Keep Clean

I brush my teeth.
I comb my hair.
I bathe my body.
I wash my hands.

We take care of

ourselves,

each other,

our community,

our country,

and our world.

Prevent Malaria

Life Cycle of a Mosquito

The full life-cycle of a mosquito takes about a month. They go through four stages of development. The four stages are egg, pupa, larva, and adult. The adult lives for only a few weeks.

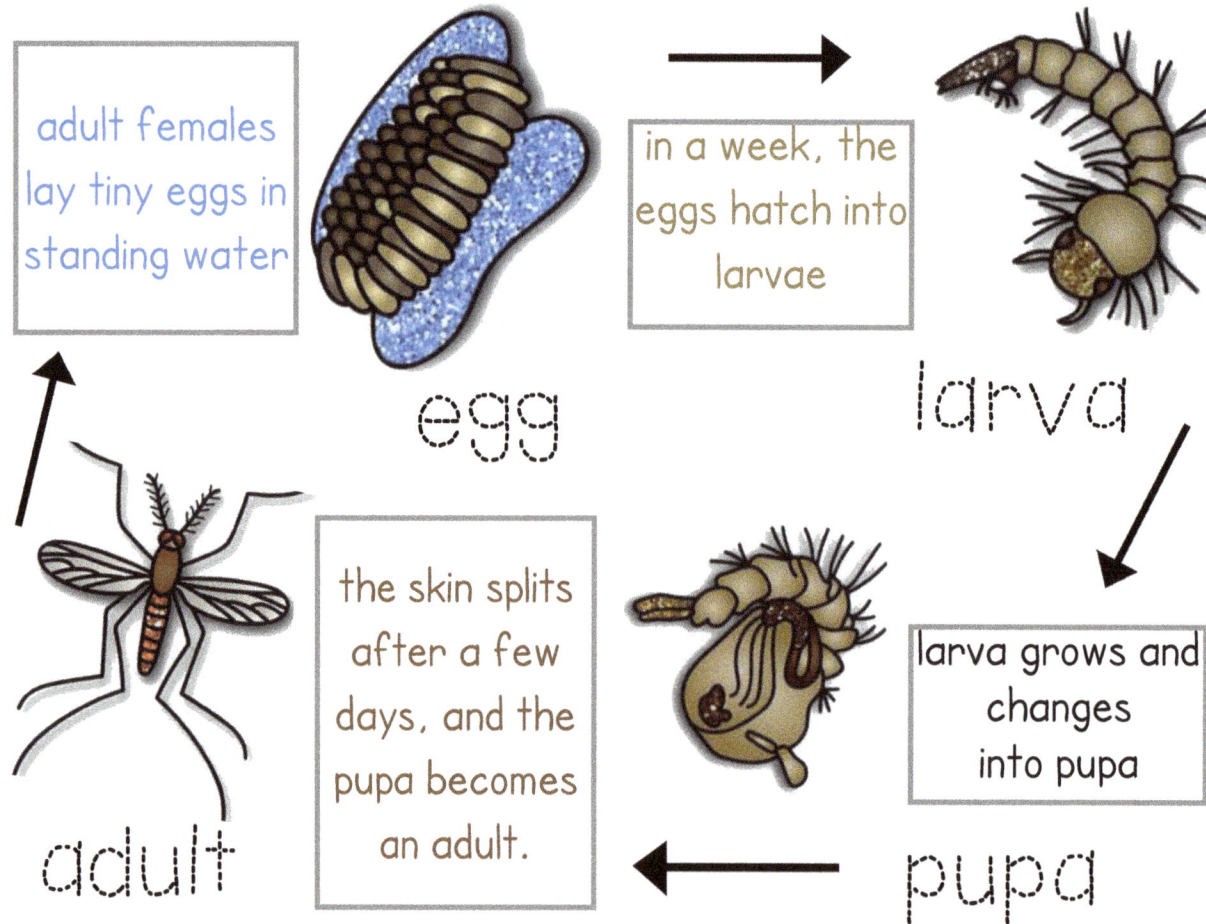

How to prevent malaria and stay well.

Always keep your home and yard clean of garbage.

Get anti-malaria medicine from your doctor.

Do not keep dirty water around.

Use mosquito net and spray to prevent bites.

5 Things I Like About Myself

1. _____

2. _____

3. _____

4. _____

5. _____

www.ingramcontent.com/pod-product-compliance
Lightning Source LLC
Chambersburg PA
CBHW051400110526
44592CB00023B/2896